I Know the Rules!

I WAIT MY TURN!

By Bray Jacobson

Gareth Stevens
PUBLISHING

Please visit our website, www.garethstevens.com. For a free color catalog of all our high-quality books, call toll free 1-800-542-2595 or fax 1-877-542-2596.

Library of Congress Cataloging-in-Publication Data

Names: Jacobson, Bray, author.
Title: I wait my turn! / Bray Jacobson.
Description: Buffalo, New York : Gareth Stevens Publishing, [2024] | Series: I know the rules! | Includes index.
Identifiers: LCCN 2022051475 (print) | LCCN 2022051476 (ebook) | ISBN 9781538286715 (library binding) | ISBN 9781538286708 (paperback) | ISBN 9781538286722 (ebook)
Subjects: LCSH: Sharing–Juvenile literature. | Courtesy–Juvenile literature.
Classification: LCC BJ1533.G4 J35 2024 (print) | LCC BJ1533.G4 (ebook) | DDC 177/.7–dc23/eng/20230118
LC record available at https://lccn.loc.gov/2022051475
LC ebook record available at https://lccn.loc.gov/2022051476

Published in 2024 by
Gareth Stevens Publishing
2544 Clinton Street
Buffalo, NY 14224

Designer: Claire Wrazin
Editor: Kristen Nelson

Photo credits: cover wavebreakmedia/Shutterstock.com; p. 5 stockfour/Shutterstock.com; pp. 7, 24 (marker) Friends Stock/Shutterstock.com; pp. 9, 11 Zurijeta/Shutterstock.com; pp. 13, 15, 17, 24 (swing) jpointstudio/Shutterstock.com; p. 19 Pixel-Shot/Shutterstock.com; pp. 21, 23 fizkes/Shutterstock.com.

Printed in the United States of America

CPSIA compliance information: Batch #CSGS24: For further information contact Gareth Stevens, at 1-800-542-2595.

Contents

I know how to wait
my turn.
It's a rule at school.

Terrance has the
blue marker.
Kara wants it.
She waits her turn.

Harvey and Daniel see a new toy car. They both want to play with it.

Harvey lets Daniel
play first.
He waits his turn.

Ruth is on the swing.
I want to swing next.

I use a calm voice.
I ask Ruth for a turn.

She swings a little more.
Then it is my turn!

We take turns at home.
Gen is watching
a show.
Robert wants to watch.

Robert asks if he can watch next.
He uses kind words.
He waits calmly.

Gen finishes her show.
It is Robert's turn!

Words to Know

marker

swing

Index